2014

W9-AQI-473

YOUR LAND AND MY LAND ASIA

We Visit

# CAMBODIA

Claire

O'Neal

Mitchell Lane
PUBLISHERS
P.O. Box 196
Hockessin, Delaware 19707

MCL FO
NEPTUNE CITY
PUBLIC LIBRARY

# YOUR LAND AND MY LAND
# ASIA

Cambodia

China

India

Indonesia

Japan

Malaysia

North Korea

The Philippines

Singapore

South Korea

YOUR LAND AND MY LAND
ASIA

We Visit

# CAMBODIA

## Mitchell Lane
### PUBLISHERS

Copyright © 2014 by Mitchell Lane Publishers, Inc. All rights reserved. No part of this book may be reproduced without written permission from the publisher. Printed and bound in the United States of America.

Printing          1          2          3          4          5          6          7          8          9

Asia

Library of Congress Cataloging-in-Publication Data
O'Neal, Claire.
  We visit Cambodia / by Claire O'Neal.
       pages cm. — (Your land and my land: Asia)
  Includes bibliographical references and index.
  ISBN 978-1-61228-475-0 (library bound)
  1.  Cambodia—Juvenile literature.  I. Title.
  DS554.3.O54 2013
  959.6—dc23
                                                      2013033970
eBook ISBN: 9781612285306

PUBLISHER'S NOTE: This story is based on the author's extensive research, which she believes to be accurate. Documentation of this research is on page 61.

   The internet sites referenced herein were active as of the publication date. Due to the fleeting nature of some websites, we cannot guarantee they will all be active when you are reading this book.

PBP

# Contents

# Introduction

Hot, wet Cambodia lies in Southeast Asia, the region south of China and east of India. Cambodia has been Asia's "Rice Bowl," feeding empires with its plentiful rice harvest since 2500 BCE. And yet, despite its fertile soil and one thousand years of culture and empire, the United Nations ranks Cambodia today as one of 50 poorest, least-developed countries in the world.[1] Cambodia works today to rebuild after 30 years of civil war, including 3½ years of genocide at the hands of the bloodthirsty Cambodian communist government, the Khmer Rouge.

Dollars from its thriving tourism industry help. Gorgeous and green, the jungle of Cambodia lies in wait like a basking cobra to strike at your heart. Millions of tourists from the world over visit the 900-year-old temple ruins of Angkor Wat, the splendor of the capital city, Phnom Penh, and the sparkling, pristine beaches along the Gulf of Thailand. Few people can experience the wonders of Cambodia and leave unchanged, especially when they see how such a long-suffering people can remain so warm, welcoming, and full of hope.

**The Angkor Wat temple complex, near Siem Reap, Cambodia**

## Asia

RUSSIA

Sea of Okhotsk

KAZAKHSTAN

MONGOLIA

GEORGIA

Caspian Sea

UZBEKISTAN

KYRGYZSTAN

Sea of Japan

ARMENIA

TURKEY

AZERBAIJAN

TURKMENISTAN

TAJIKISTAN

N. KOREA

S. KOREA

JAPAN

Mediterranean Sea

SYRIA

LEBANON

IRAN

AFGHANISTAN

CHINA

ISRAEL

IRAQ

East China Sea

JORDAN

KUWWAIT

Persian Gulf

PAKISTAN

NEPAL

BHUTAN

BAHRAIN

QATAR

UNITED ARAB

EMIRATES

INDIA

BANGLADESH

TAIWAN

SAUDI

ARABIA

OMAN

MYAN-MAR

LAOS

VIETNAM

Red Sea

YEMEN

Arabian Sea

Bay of Bengal

THAI-LAND

CAMBODIA

South China Sea

PHILIPPINES

Philippine Sea

Gulf of Aden

Andaman Sea

MALDIVES

SRI LANKA

BRUNEI

MALAYSIA

SINGAPORE

North Pacific Ocean

Indian Ocean

1200 Kilometers

1200 Miles

INDONESIA

EAST TIMOR

Traditional Khmer architecture makes the Independence Monument (Vimean Ekareach) stand out in modern Phnom Penh, Cambodia. Built in 1958, the monument commemorates Cambodia's independence from France.

# The People
# of the Naga

Once upon a time, a handsome Asian prince named Preah Thong set out to make a life on his own. The adventurous prince had heard fascinating tales of the Naga, a mysterious and serpent-like people who lived in a faraway watery land. He hoped to conquer them and build a new kingdom. Preah Thong boarded a royal boat and commanded his 6,000 oarsmen to journey to the murky, jungled Naga lands. As they drew near, the prince saw a beautiful woman standing on the shore. Instantly, Preah Thong's heart was conquered by love. The woman happily shared Preah Thong's feelings. But she was the Naga princess, Neang Neak. What would happen when they told her father, the king, a terrible and deadly cobra with seven heads?[1] They simply showed the king that their love was true. The fierce king gave the lovers his blessing. As a wedding gift, he also gave them a home. He used his seven mouths to suck all the water away from the Naga kingdom so his daughter's husband could rule on dry land. The land became Kambuja—later, Cambodia—and the many children of the marriage became the ancestors of all Cambodians.

Today, Cambodians pay homage to this legend by calling themselves the People of the Naga. But Cambodia's actual origin remains a mystery. No one is sure if Cambodia's early people migrated from China, or India, or from the islands of Southeast Asia. By 4200 BCE, however, the first settlers had made their homes in caves like Laang Spean ("Cave of Bridges"), located in the Battambang province in western Cambodia. They were the first members of the Khmer race,

**Cambodian farmers rely on water buffalo to help plow their flooded rice fields.**

the ethnic group that composes over 90% of Cambodia's people.

Change is slow to come in Cambodia, as if the thick and misty rainforest jungle has the power to make time stand still. Though the Khmer spread out, and civilizations and wars came and went, people continued to use caves as homes until the 9th century CE.[2] Rice was introduced to the wet and fertile Tonle Sap lake region in central Cambodia around 2500 BCE, and it continues to power the economy. Most important to the Khmer people are their shared, deep roots—faith in Theravada Buddhism, the Khmer language, and their long-reigning royal family. A bowl of fish and rice or a graceful traditional dance will make any Cambodian flash an easy grin.

But peek underneath the friendly people and the land's lush year-round green, and you'll find a country struggling to move beyond its violent past. Civil war and government corruption have held the country hostage since 1970. As leaders wrestled for power with help from their foreign friends, Cambodian rice farmers paid the bloody

**FYI FACT:**

Cambodians tell the story of Preah Thong and Neang Neak through a classical dance called the Ramvong. While oboes, wooden flutes, violins, drums, and xylophones set the mood, dancers in elaborate costumes move slowly, making delicate shapes with their hands and bodies. Professional performers train for years. At home, Cambodians dance the Ramvong with friends and family.

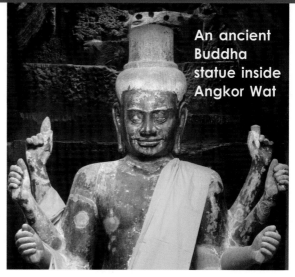

An ancient Buddha statue inside Angkor Wat

price. Between 1970 and 1975, dictator Pol Pot ordered the execution of anyone educated or skilled, or even those who looked different or odd. His Khmer Rouge carried out a horrifying genocide that killed 1.7 million Cambodians between 1975 and 1979. By 1977, the average life span of a Cambodian plummeted to only 32 years.[3] Bitter politics throughout the 1980s and 1990s kept the violence going. Only recently, under longstanding Prime Minister Hun Sen and King Norodom Sihamoni, has Cambodia's government been stable enough to focus on improving the lives of its people.

Though the average life span has nearly doubled over the last 35 years, the country faces many challenges. It is one of the poorest countries in Asia, where 2.7 million people—nearly 20% of the population—live on less than $1.25 per day.[4] Almost 40% percent of Cambodian children under the age of five do not get enough food.[5] Over half of the population is less than 25 years old, and most have little to no education or job opportunities. The politicians and new businessmen who do, live a western style of life in the bustling cities of Siem Reap, Battambang, and especially the noisy, sprawling capital city of Phnom Penh. But 80% of Cambodia's 14.3 million people live just as their ancestors have for thousands of years. In quiet, scattered villages of 100 to 400 people, they barely survive with the rice they grow or the fish they catch. Today, Cambodia tells a tale of two countries. The rich in the cities get richer, and the poor country farmers have no choice but to get poorer. But together, all Cambodians have survived horror and tragedy in the land of their ancestors with *penh jut*—a heart full of hope. Can their ancient beliefs and cherished customs bring them a better life in a modern world?

## CAMBODIA FACTS AT A GLANCE

**Official Country Name:** Kingdom of Cambodia
**Official Language:** Khmer; French and English are also spoken
**Population:** 15,205,539 (July 2013 estimate)
**Land Area:** 69,898 square miles (181,035 square kilometers); roughly the size of Missouri
**Capital:** Phnom Penh
**Government:** Unitary parliamentary constitutional monarchy
**Ethnic Makeup:** Khmer (90 percent), Vietnamese (5 percent), Chinese (1 percent), Cham (1.5 percent), other (4 percent)
**Religions:** Theravada Buddhism (official, more than 95 percent)
**Exports:** Clothing and footwear, wood, rice, rubber, fish, tobacco
**Imports:** Oil, cigarettes, gold, construction materials, machinery and cars, medicines
**Crops:** Rice, rubber, vegetables, cashews, cassava, fish
**Average Temperatures:** hottest in April, average high 95°F (35°C); coldest in January, average low 69°F (20°C)
**Average Annual Rainfall:** 63.7 inches (162 centimeters)
**Highest Point:** Phnom Aural — 5,938 feet (1,810 meters)
**Longest River:** Mekong River — 480 miles (772 kilometers)
**National Flag:** Cambodia's flag was first used from 1948-1970, and again from 1993 until today. Its blue stripes symbolize liberty, with red in the center for the bravery of its people. At its heart is Angkor Wat, depicted in white, to celebrate the religious heritage of the Cambodian people.
**National Flower:** Romduol *(Mitrella mesnyi)*
**National Bird:** Giant ibis (*Thaumatibis gigantea*)
**National Tree:** Cambodian palm (*Borassus flabellifer*)
**Currency:** Riel
**Provinces** *(khaet)*: 23, with 1 municipality (Phnom Penh)
**National symbol:** Royal Coat of Arms
**National anthem:** "Nokor Reach" ("Majestic Kingdom")
**National motto:** "Nation, Religion, King"
**National fruit:** Chicken-egg banana (*Musa aromatica*)
**National mammal:** Kouprey (Bos sauveli)
**National reptile:** Royal turtle (Batagur affinis)
**National fish:** Giant barb (Catlocarpio siamensis)

Source: CIA World Factbook, Cambodia, October 25, 2013.
Weatherbase.com, Cambodia.
Norodom Sihamoni, "Royal Decree on Designation of Animals and Plants as National Symbols of the Kingdom of Cambodia," March 21, 2005.

Beautiful Kep Beach is a popular destination for locals and tourists alike. This quiet coastal resort attracts swimmers, bird watchers, and seafood lovers.

# Geography

Heart-shaped Cambodia is the smallest country in mainland Southeast Asia. It has a land area of 69,898 square miles (181,035 square kilometers), approximately the size of Missouri. It shares borders with Thailand in the west and northwest, Laos in the northeast, and Vietnam in the east. Cambodia has one coastline, a 275-mile (443-kilometer) gem that sparkles with crystal blue waters and white sands in the southwest along the Gulf of Thailand.

Most of Cambodia is a flat, fertile plain, ringed by mountains in the north and southwest. The low Dangrek Mountains ("Carrying-Pole" in Khmer) stretch along Cambodia's northern border, from the Mekong River in Laos to Thailand's highlands. The scenic Damrei ("Elephant") Mountains run from the coastline at Kampot in a short, slender, north-south line. They connect to, and form a continuous range with, the Kravanh ("Cardamom") Mountains, a larger range that frames the coast before crossing the Thai border. Cambodia's highest peak, Phnom Aural, rises 5,940 feet (1,810 meters) on the eastern edge of the Cardamom Range near Kampong. The Koh Kong Conservation Corridor around Phnom Aural preserves the unique plants and animals that live in Cambodia's mountain rainforests, including endangered species like the Indochinese tiger, clouded leopard, and the Sunda pangolin.

Cambodia's tropical latitude makes it hot year-round. Temperatures in Phnom Penh average between lows of 71°F (22°C) in December

The Dangrek Mountains form a natural border with Thailand. The highest point is 2,470 feet (753 meters).

and highs of 95°F (35°C) in April. Monsoons define Cambodia's seasons. Wet winds blow in from the Gulf of Thailand in June, carrying monsoon rains that fall in intense showers for several hours every day. October, the wettest month, averages only 7 dry days in Phnom Penh.[1] The winds change course in mid-November, bringing relief with drier, cooler air. Westerners generally travel to Cambodia during the milder dry season, especially between November and February. Those who brave the afternoon storms of the monsoon get to watch the jungle awakening with green, the rice paddies sprouting fresh shoots, and the moss and lichen plastering Angkor Wat with life. The monsoon season also fills out the streams so that Cambodians can travel by boat, the preferred method of transportation for many of them.

This rain drains into the Mekong River, which flows north to south through Cambodia as a wide, muddy gash. The Mekong combines with the Tonle Sap River at Cambodia's capital city, Phnom Penh. Together the waters grow into a broad, single stream that continues out of Cambodia, flooding the marshy Mekong Delta in Vietnam before emptying into the South China Sea. The Mekong River Basin contains rich biodiversity, second only to the Amazon. The greatest number of species of large freshwater fish in the world live here, from the Siamese giant carp to the Mekong freshwater stingray. The Irrawaddy dolphin, a freshwater species, also swims in the Mekong.

Cambodia boasts the largest freshwater lake in Southeast Asia, the Tonle Sap ("Great Lake"). Most Cambodians live in this region, where floods renew the wet, rich land each year. The lake grows and shrinks in a monsoon rhythm. In the dry season, it has an area of about 1,042 square miles (2,700 square kilometers), as the Tonle Sap River carries water away from the lake towards the Mekong River. During the monsoon season, the level of the Mekong rises higher than the lake.

2

**FYI FACT:**

Rubber trees thrive in Indochina, but are not a native species. In colonial times, the British brought rubber trees from the Amazon to the rainforests of Southeast Asia. Today, rubber is one of Cambodia's most important exports.

Gravity pulls the waters of the Mekong backwards, carrying the water into the Tonle Sap. The lake swells to nearly 6,200 square miles (16,000 square kilometers), spilling over its banks and covering the soil with fresh sediment from the Mekong Delta. Cambodians celebrate this unusual reversal with Bon Om Touk, a national water festival in November featuring three days of fun, with fireworks, dancing, canoe races, and more.

Over 75% of Cambodia was once covered by forests and woodlands. These areas have been slashed to half their original size. Deforestation affects Cambodia's fresh fish supply, since many species spawn in the natural hiding places created by water-loving, tangled tree roots like the mangrove. The severity of flooding also increases during the rainy season without trees to stabilize riverbanks. Many areas have been devastated by logging, an easy way for Cambodia's peasant farmers to earn a little extra cash. They sell valuable hardwood trees such as teak and mahogany—often illegally—at the Thai border. In turn, this wood is sold to wealthier countries for furniture or flooring. In some cases, forested areas have been cleared for farming or replanted with rubber trees.

Cambodia's top cash crop—rice—is also eaten at every meal. Farms like this one in northern Cambodia can grow rice of different varieties year-round.

# Ancient History to Independence

Cambodian history begins around 2500 BCE, when the Chinese first brought rice plants to Southeast Asia. Rice farmers chopped down Cambodia's thick jungle trees to make way for this new and important food source. By 600 BCE, Cambodians were using iron tools, like buffalo-pulled metal plows, for rice planting and harvesting. Over time, farmers and fishermen settled into villages near each other to share work animals, tools, and crops.

Cambodian villages found new roles as trading posts once other civilizations came exploring. When Chinese adventurers visited the Mekong Delta around the 1st century, they encountered kings and queens who rode on elephants and kept many slaves to build their wooden palaces. What the Chinese called the Kingdom of Funan stretched across the southern parts of modern-day Cambodia, Vietnam, and Thailand. The people of Funan farmed or worked as craftsmen or expert engineers who built canals to deliver water to rice fields. Funan also kept Cambodia's first written records. The kingdom fell to the short-lived kingdom of Chenla in the 6th century.

These early kingdoms' names came from China, but Cambodian culture was also strongly shaped by influences from India. By 600 CE, Cambodians had borrowed heavily from India's Sanskrit language to craft a language of their own—known as Khmer—for speaking and writing.[1] Hinduism, India's main religion, captured the Khmer imagination with its colorful parade of romantic and violent gods and goddesses. Tales of the all-powerful Hindu god-kings Shiva and Vishnu

**Elaborate stone carvings of gods and goddesses, kings and mythological beings, line the 900-year-old walls of the temple of Angkor Wat.**

may have been spun by conquering warriors from the nearby Kingdom of Champa, a Hindu empire based in Vietnam between the 2nd and 8th centuries. Champa waged constant war along the coasts of Southeast Asia. Cambodian villagers blended classic Indian legends with animism, a folk religion with beliefs in magic and animal gods. After Buddhism arose around the 5th century BCE in northern India, it slowly trickled throughout Southeast Asia. But it took centuries for Buddhism's quiet seed to grow to become the way of life that it is in modern Cambodia.

Cambodia's first strong, homegrown kingdom arose on the banks of the Tonle Sap in Cambodia's northwest region. In 802, Jayavarman II declared himself king in a sacred ceremony on the top of Phnom Kulen ("Phnom" is Khmer for "mountain," so the name means "Mountain of Lychee Fruits"). Borrowing from Hindu myth,

Jayavarman II proclaimed that he and his family had the right to rule forever because they were descended from gods. Jayavarman and his many descendants formed the Khmer Empire. At its height in the 12th century, the empire controlled all of what is now Cambodia as well as most of Thailand, Laos, and Vietnam.

The Khmer Empire built its greatness on rice. In the 9th century, King Indravarman I oversaw the construction of enormous irrigation projects that brought water from the Tonle Sap to thirsty rice fields, allowing farmers to harvest rice up to three times per year.[2] Armies of slaves constructed canals near the capital at Angkor that snaked through the jungle. The fertile Angkor—which sprawled over nearly 400 square miles (1,000 square km)—became the largest human settlement before the Industrial Revolution, over 500 years later.[3] Fueled by rice and the many slaves captured from their wars, Suryavarman II and his successor Jayavaraman VII began massive temple-building projects throughout the realm—especially at Angkor—in the 12th century. Many of these temples still stand, including the magnificent temple complex at Angkor Wat, near the modern-day town of Siem Reap. The site contains over 200 acres of ornately carved and decorated temples, guarded by a wide moat. Suryavarman II originally designed the wat—which means "temple" in Khmer—to serve as his larger-than-life grave. His builders crafted the central tower complex to symbolize the sacred Hindu mountain, Mount Meru. Detailed sandstone panels with carved pictures of Hindu folktales form walls around sculptures of stone hydra-headed stone snakes—a nod to the Naga legends.

**FYI FACT:**

Though Angkor Wat was originally decorated to honor Hindu gods, Buddhist King Jayavarman VII (who reigned c.1181 to 1218) added sculptures of the Buddha throughout the grounds. Since 1432, the temple has been cared for by Buddhist monks.

**The streets of Phnom Penh are a mix of old and new. Modern apartments share space with 100-year-old buildings from the time when France ruled Cambodia.**

After the death of Jayavarman VII around 1215, the Khmer Empire faded quickly. Khmer territory shrank as its neighbors grew in power. The kingdom of Ayutthaya to the west (in modern-day Thailand) conquered Angkor's capital in 1431 and went on to claim most of modern-day Cambodia by the 16th century. The Kingdom of Champa, in modern-day Vietnam, invaded from the east in the 17th century and controlled the southeast and the Mekong Delta. The Khmer people often suffered, or were slaughtered, at the hands of these invaders. They grew to hate the Thai and the Vietnamese, feelings that still seethe in Cambodia today.

In the 19th century, European powers turned their colony-building eyes towards Asia. Cambodia's King Norodom I (who ruled from 1860 to 1904) actually invited France in, signing away his kingdom to the French in 1863. Shrewd Norodom knew that French rule would protect the Cambodian people and their way of life from being swallowed up by Vietnam and Ayutthaya. In return, Cambodia had to make some important changes. French governors abolished slavery in 1884. They introduced the French language, culture, and cooking. They also took away much of the king's power. Si Votha, the king's half-brother, quickly gathered supporters to drive the French out. The French retaliated mercilessly, and removed weapons from the population to prevent further rebellion.

Most Cambodians were poor, uneducated rice farmers who could care less. Their life of growing rice in small villages, bullied by a government that demanded its share, continued almost unchanged under the French. But as wealthier families became educated in French schools, they grew angry that Western ideas of democracy and independence did not seem to apply to their home country. By the 1930s, the newly educated Cambodians printed their own newspapers, with angry words against the French.

In 1940, France's hold on power slipped as their homeland fell under the control of the German army in World War II. Japanese troops moved into Cambodia in 1941, claiming it and much of Southeast Asia as part of the Empire of Japan. Cambodia's throne changed hands, too. When King Sisowath Monivong died that same year, France crowned his grandson, Norodom Sihanouk, king. The Japanese forced Sihanouk to declare his country independent from France in 1945 and the Kingdom of Kampuchea was born. The French resumed control only five months later with Japan's defeat in World War II. But hopes of liberty had taken hold among Cambodia's educated elite. The French reluctantly but peacefully gave Cambodia its independence on November 9, 1953.

As Queen Monineath looks on, Cambodian King Norodom Sihanouk and a schoolgirl release a bird during an Independence Day celebration. Cambodia celebrates this holiday on November 9, the anniversary of its independence from France.

# Modern History

The new Kingdom of Cambodia became a constitutional monarchy, with Norodom Sihanouk as king. Cambodians adored Sihanouk. As an actual descendant of Jayavarman VII, he symbolized the country's glorious past, now alive in the present. Like the former Khmer god-kings, Cambodians literally allowed Sihanouk to get away with murder. When political opponents accused Sihanouk of pocketing tax money and jailing those who questioned him, they often met with a bloody end. Corruption at all levels in the government was not only taken for granted, it was expected. Cambodians had spent their country's history under one ruler after another who helped themselves to the people's land and rice. As a popular Khmer proverb suggests, "If you have money you have a good heart. If you are poor you must have a bad heart."[1] In other words, the rich and powerful deserve to get richer, while it is the fate of the poor to endure a lifetime of suffering.

In 1954, Cambodia's neighbor Vietnam erupted in a civil war that pitted South Vietnam against the communist Viet Cong, who were supported by North Vietnam. Sihanouk insisted that Cambodia should stay out of the fight. But his weak military could do little to stop the Viet Cong from smuggling weapons and troops through Cambodia's loose borders. A high-ranking army officer, Lon Nol, wanted the Viet Cong and North Vietnamese out of Cambodia. He staged a coup d'etat on March 12, 1970, while the king indulged in a lavish Paris vacation. As president of the new Khmer Republic, Lon Nol sent his soldiers to fight against the Viet Cong, and allowed American troops into

Cambodia to help. But he was unpopular, and a civil war began. He and his troops battled Cambodians loyal to the ousted royal family. They found themselves outmaneuvered by guerilla warriors trained by the mysterious Khmer Rouge, a communist group of Cambodians arising out of the jungle.

The Khmer Rouge steadily gained supporters influence throughout Cambodia's farming villages and small towns. On April 17, 1975, the Khmer Rouge entered Phnom Penh. Lon Nol fled for his life. The capital city erupted in cheers to welcome the Khmer Rouge and waved white flags in hopes of peace.

Pol Pot (shown here as a young man)

**FYI FACT:**

Pol Pot described land mines as "perfect soldiers," lying in wait until, triggered by the pressure of a footstep, they explode. Millions of them continue to threaten safety and progress in Cambodia today. Most victims are farmers trying to clear new land, hungry villagers foraging for food, or children out exploring.

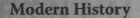
4

**Some of the people displaced from their homes in Phonm Penh immediately after the Khmer Rouge takeover begin their long trek into the rice fields. By 1979, as many as three million Cambodians had died from overwork, starvation, and disease.**

These hopes were quickly dashed. The new leader, Pol Pot, had a plan to create a farm-based society. He would bring Cambodia back to its simple roots, starting over from the new "Year Zero." Within hours after taking control, young Khmer Rouge soldiers went door-to-door. They explained to each surprised family that they must give up their house, their cars, all their possessions, and walk to the rice fields in rural Cambodia, sometimes hundreds of miles away, to begin new lives as farmers. Those who refused were immediately shot dead.

The Khmer Rouge government broke all contact with the outside world, and then looked inward for enemies. Pol Pot targeted huge groups of Cambodians for execution: government workers, soldiers, policemen, businessmen, teachers, doctors, monks, even people who

**The United States used Cambodian air space and ground bases to launch attacks into Vietnam during the Vietnam War.**

wore glasses or could read. To the Khmer Rouge, the perfect Cambodian citizen was a simple peasant farmer. Educated people or city dwellers were not to be trusted. They had lived among Cambodia's enemies—the French, the Vietnamese, the Thai—and could have been brainwashed by them. Pol Pot's slogan reminded everyone that "To keep you is no benefit, to kill you is no loss." Fathers, mothers, even children were imprisoned on trumped-up charges and tortured, or simply shot. In the rice fields, anyone could be led away from their backbreaking work at any time and clubbed to death, their bodies left in piles to rot.

The three-and-a-half-year genocide of the Khmer Rouge took the lives of as many as 3 million people—nearly two out of every five Cambodians—essentially eliminating an entire generation. Those who survived existed in horrible conditions, afraid of starvation and death. Without teachers to educate them, businessmen to build an economy,

The Khmer Rouge buried nearly 9,000 Cambodians in a pile at the Choeung Ek Killing Fields. A pile of human skulls there today stands as a dark reminder of Cambodia's past.

troops to protect them, or doctors and nurses to heal them from the widespread disease and starvation brought about by overwork and food shortages, Cambodians no longer had hope. Even their beloved Buddhist religion was banned, leaving Cambodians unable even to mourn their dead.

In December 1978, a strong and newly united Vietnam invaded Cambodia and easily pushed the Khmer Rouge from power. Pol Pot's weakened forces scattered and fled. At first, Western nations condemned Vietnam's move. But without the Khmer Rouge, Cambodians were free to leave their forced-labor camps. Thousands made their way on foot to the Thai border, rail-thin, injured, and near death. Reporters from around the world learned the truth behind the silence of the Khmer Rouge.

The Vietnamese pulled out in 1989 and left a communist-friendly Cambodian named Hun Sen in charge as prime minister. But without Vietnam's strong forces to keep order, guns flashed on the streets of Phnom Penh like fish in the Mekong. Hun Sen and his Communist People's Party (CPP) fought those loyal to King Sihanouk, while the Khmer Rouge lashed out from their western stronghold at the diamond mines in Pailin. International news told of drive-by shootings, grenades launched into crowds at political rallies, and assassination attempts on politicians or their bodyguards. Once again, ordinary Cambodians were caught in the crossfire, left helpless and afraid.

Cambodia's beloved former king Norodom Sihanouk died on October 15, 2012, at age 89. At his funeral on February 4, 2013, tens of thousands of mourners lined the streets of Phnom Penh to see his golden coffin and chariot, as well as a half-mile-long parade of royal dancers.

# Chapter 5

# Government and Politics

The outside world refused to stand by and watch the Cambodian people again become victims of their own government. Cambodia's infighting leaders reluctantly agreed to hand over control of their country to the United Nations at the Paris Peace Agreements on October 23, 1991. Over the next two years, the U.N. spent $3 billion to send 16,000 peacekeeping troops and 5,000 civil administrators to Cambodia. They crafted a modern constitution that guaranteed basic human rights and a democratically elected government.[1]

Free elections held in 1993 seemed to be a great success. Ninety percent of Cambodians voted, choosing Ranariddh Sihanouk—King Sihanouk's son—as prime minister. Hun Sen was furious. He refused to accept the results of the election. King Sihanouk was also furious; he demanded to be installed as king once more. The U.N. helped the three parties reach an agreement. Sihanouk would return as king, but with few powers. Ranariddh and Hun Sen would share the position of prime minister. The National Assembly, elected to represent the provinces of Cambodia, approved a constitution that created a parliamentary monarchy known as the Kingdom of Cambodia.

On the surface, the Kingdom of Cambodia is a stable democracy. Cambodia's monarchy is one of the oldest in the world, continuously in power between 550 and 1970. The people adored their kings as proud symbols of Khmer history. When Norodom Sihanouk died in October 2012, his subjects mourned for days, even though he had not been king for eight years. His son, Norodom Sihamoni, reigns today, having taken his father's place in a peaceful transition in 2004.

The monarchy has only limited powers in Cambodia, where real power lies in the hands of ministers elected to Cambodia's two-branch parliament. The National Assembly consists of 123 members, elected every five years to represent each of Cambodia's 23 provinces and the special administrative area of Phnom Penh. The Senate has 58 members, 54 elected by leaders of the provinces, two more hand-picked by the king, and another two chosen by members of the National Assembly. The party with the most members in the National Assembly chooses a prime minister from among themselves to serve as Cambodia's official Head of State, but Hun Sen has held this position in one way or another since 1985. National elections every five years since 1998 have kept Hun Sen's Communist People's Party in charge. Hun Sen claims that his stability as a ruler helps rebuild a Cambodia still in tatters from the civil wars of the 1970s.

In practice, Cambodia is ranked as one of the top 20 most corrupt countries in the world.[2] International observers accuse Hun Sen of acting like a dictator, lining his pockets with money from the billions of dollars in foreign aid donated by other countries to help his country's poor. Sam Rainsy, Cambodia's most promising opposition candidate, worries that Hun Sen creates a culture of fear, where elections can never be fair when those who oppose Hun Sen face bullying, jail, or worse. Rainsy himself fled the country in 2005 when Hun Sen threatened him with jail time on made-up charges. In March 2013,

**FYI FACT:**

Cambodia's current flag was readopted in 1993, after the UN-sponsored elections. King Sihanouk had used the same flag during his rule between 1948 and 1970. Cambodia and Afghanistan are the only countries in the world with flags that feature pictures of buildings.

**Cambodian Prime Minister Hun Sen (right) hosts then-U.S. Secretary of State Hillary Clinton (left) in Phnom Penh in 2012.**

foreign observers again groaned their disapproval when Hun Sen nominated his own son and the sons of other members of the CCP for prominent government roles in upcoming elections, all in the name of maintaining stability.[3]

Rainsy returned to Cambodia in 2013, thanks to a pardon from King Sihamoni, to help the opposition party in the elections. Hun Sen's CPP party claimed yet another victory, but this time by its narrowest margin ever. The military moved into Phnom Penh as Rainsy and the Cambodia National Rescue Party (CNRP) announced they would hold massive protests to open the Cambodian people's eyes to widespread election fraud, and to the growing fear that Hun Sen and the CPP were scheming to make themselves into a new dynasty of all-powerful rulers for Cambodia.

The ancient stone wonders of Angkor Wat represent a masterpiece of Khmer art and architecture. Protected as a UNESCO World Heritage Site since 1994, Angkor Wat today is one of the largest archaeological sites in the world.

# Resources and Jobs

Despite Hun Sen's corruption, the stability of his constant rule has fueled an explosion in Cambodia's economy. The country's revenue grew almost 10% each year from 2004 until the global recession in 2008.[1] Tourism is the hottest new industry. The exotic jungle ruins of Angkor Wat beckoned fearless travelers after French explorer Henri Mouhot became the first European to visit them in 1860. A modern audience has rediscovered its wonders. Tourists flock to the grandeur of Phnom Penh before heading to resort towns on the beach and luxury hotels near mysterious temple ruins. In 2012, over 3.5 million tourists paid more than $2 billion to see Cambodia's national treasures for themselves.[2]

Cambodia's clothing industry also bursts at the seams with new urban jobs. The legendary silk weaving of the Cambodian people has attracted the attention of international companies like H&M, Adidas, and Gap, who employ over 400,000 Cambodian workers in clothing factories.[3] International human rights groups have called the factories "sweatshops," reporting that working conditions include long hours, minimal vacation time, and pressure to work ever harder and faster. But many Cambodians feel lucky to have a job in a factory paying $60-$90 per month, 50% more than the average Cambodian's wages.[4]

In the country, rice is still king. Agriculture provided 36% of the country's revenue in 2012.[5] Farmers use nearly one-fourth of Cambodia's land, mostly to farm rice to feed themselves. Cambodia's waters also provide an important source of meat like fish, snake, or turtle from the Mekong or Tonle Sap, or crab or squid from the coastline for people to eat or sell.

What lies under Cambodia's soil may hold even more promise. The Kampong Thum province in central Cambodia sits on large deposits of iron and manganese ores, while gold and silver can be found in small deposits throughout the country. The Cardamom Range is known for precious gems like rubies, sapphires, and diamonds. The U.S. oil company Chevron struck oil in 2005 in the Gulf of Thailand, about 100 miles off the coast. Chevron first estimated that the large, 400-million-barrel oil deposits would fetch as much as $1.7 billion per year on the oil market, enough to more than pay for Cambodia's entire national budget in 2008.[6] Only time will tell if the new oil riches will pave a path to prosperity for all Cambodians, or just make Hun Sen and his friends richer and more powerful.

Cambodia's exciting recent growth gives hope for what the future holds. However, opportunity sharply divides the country into clear groups of haves—like politicians, businessmen, and foreign tourists—and have-nots like everybody else. Though 11 million of Cambodia's 14.3 million people are poor villagers, their government ignores their basic needs. Running water, flushing toilets, and other luxuries of modern plumbing can only be found in the richest homes, or in hotels that cater to foreigners. More than 80% of rural homes, and nearly one-quarter of urban ones, have ditch toilets and get water from hand-dug wells or local streams or lakes.[7] Clean drinking water is not available in 42% of the countryside.[8] As a result, Cambodians frequently suffer from diseases like diarrhea, cholera, typhoid fever, dysentery, and intestinal parasites virtually unknown in areas of the world where flush toilets and proper hand washing are taken for granted. Because of the hot and humid landscape, mosquito-borne diseases like malaria, dengue fever, and encephalitis also afflict Cambodians. Thanks to disease and poor access to food, one in 10 Cambodian children will not survive to age 5, and nearly 30% of those who do are malnourished, their growth and development stunted.

Worldwide, countries and charities have been moved by the heartbreaking plight of the Cambodian poor. Big-budget outside donors

**Workers from the non-governmental organization (NGO) Trailblazer Foundation deliver equipment to help villagers near Siem Reap purify their water.**

like the World Bank and the International Monetary Fund sponsor large-scale projects such as road-building, while small non-governmental organizations (NGOs)—non-profit charities from foreign countries—supply money and personnel to help with everything from clearing fields of land mines to teaching job skills and providing medicine. From 1998 to 2007, foreign charities donated $5.5 billion to Cambodia.[9]

With friends like these, Hun Sen can use this international aid to pay for half of Cambodia's budget—everything from health care to education and transportation, even paying lawmakers' salaries. No one knows exactly how much foreign aid Cambodia's poor families actually see. While some wish for an easier life, many simply carry on, living in much the same way that worked for their Khmer ancestors for the past 1,000 years.

FYI FACT:

So many U.S. dollars changed hands during the U.N. occupation of 1992-1993 that Cambodians now prefer using American money as their currency. They make small change using the Cambodian riel note, at the rate of about 4,000 riels to one dollar.[10]

Buddhist monks wear robes and shave their heads to honor Buddha's simple way of life. Southeast Asian monks often wear orange, after the ancient practice of using the herb saffron to dye robes.

# Religion and Holidays

Cambodians are working to rebuild their strong Buddhist heritage. The Khmer Rouge killed monks and destroyed anything that bound Cambodians to religion—written records, libraries, monasteries, temples, and shrines. Once the Khmer Rouge fell from power, Cambodians rushed to rebuild wats, or Buddhist temples. People donated furniture or made statues and paintings themselves. Even the most impoverished Cambodians gave money on holy days.[1] Today, Buddhism continues to fill Cambodian's hearts with peace and hope. Theravada Buddhism is such an important part of Cambodians' national identity—96.4% of Cambodians practice the faith—that it was recognized as the official state religion in 1989.

Theravada Buddhism is the oldest and most conservative sect of Buddhism, practiced by over 150 million believers worldwide. They and other Buddhists follow the teachings of Buddhas. These are holy people who have reached nirvana, the highest state of awareness of the universe that brings inner peace and joy. The most famous Buddha was the Gautama Buddha, who lived in present-day northern India in the 5th century BCE. He began life as a pampered prince, but left everything behind—power, riches, a beautiful palace, even his wife and infant son—to meditate on the meaning of life. He found that he could overcome suffering, not just within himself, but also in the world, with thoughtful and generous words and deeds. Gautama Buddha and his closest followers shared their new understanding with others through teachings, or dharma, that were eventually written down in the Tipitaka ("three baskets").

In Cambodia, Buddhist monks are highly respected as important teachers and leaders who support everyone in the sangha, or Buddhist community. Monks generously share their food, money, skills, and knowledge with anyone in need. They staff the local Buddhist wats, important places of peace and learning. Theravada Buddhists believe that only monks can achieve enlightenment by devoting themselves to study and meditation on the dharma. Cambodians also strongly encourage their sons to serve in a wat as novice monks for at least three months, in part because monkhood may be the best chance a Cambodian boy has at an education.

Buddhists everywhere cherish their religious holidays as times of tradition and community. Buddhist New Year is celebrated every year for three days, beginning with the first full moon of April. The faithful wash statues of Buddha to symbolize purity and a fresh start. On the first full moon of May, the holiday of Visaka remembers the life of Gautama Buddha. The faithful bring caged birds or caught fish to symbolize Buddha's love of all living things. Cambodian Buddhists have a special national holiday, Pchum Ben, or "Ancestor's Day," to honor the dead as far back as seven generations. The living earn favor from their dead relatives by praying at seven pagodas, or by performing seven good deeds.[2] On Buddhist holidays throughout the year, Cambodians visit their wat to chant and meditate and make offerings of food and money to the monks and the poor.

Cambodians also enjoy government holidays throughout the year. Constitution Day on September 24 celebrates the signing of the current Cambodian constitution by King Sihanouk in 1993. Independence Day, held on November 9, honors Cambodia's independence from France in 1953. Hun Sen's Communist People's Party declared January 7 a national holiday, known as Victory Day or Liberation Day, to commemorate when the Vietnamese invaded in 1979 and removed the Khmer Rouge from power. The opposition party argues that this day should be celebrated on October 23, to commemorate the signing of the Paris Peace Agreements in 1991. Cambodians adore their

Cham people form a small but important minority in Cambodia. Most live in about 400 small villages just north of Phnom Penh, but some live on boats in the Mekong and Tonle Sap Rivers.

royal family, so much so that the royals' birthdays are national holidays. King Sihamoni's birthday on May 14 stretches out into a three-day celebration.

Throughout the years of violence, war, and unrest, a deep sense of belonging and unity has united the Khmers and kept them going. They are mostly tolerant, but do not feel the same kind of loyalty to minority ethnic groups, which include settlers from neighbor (and sometimes invader) Vietnam (5% of the population), and also ethnic Chinese (1%). The Cham people form an isolated minority group within Cambodia. The Cham live mostly in the Kampong Cham province. They speak Cham, which finds more common roots with the languages of Malaysia and Polynesian islands than it does with Khmer. The Cham descend from the peoples of the Kingdom of Champa, which claimed territory in Southeast Asia, especially Vietnam, between the 7th and 15th centuries. Most Cham also practice Islam. These differences marked them for destruction by the Khmer Rouge, with an estimated 500,000 Cham killed.

**FYI FACT:**

Many Cambodians believe in magic and in good and evil spirits. Villagers seek out sorcerers, or kru, to cure sickness and make protective charms. They also commonly ask the advice of fortunetellers before making important decisions.

Cambodian children love school and learning. They go to school for a half-day every day except Sunday. Most students help out at home or on the family farm during the rest of the day, while wealthier students pay to take extra classes.

# Chapter 8

## Language and Learning

The official language of Cambodia is Khmer, an ancient language spoken by tens of millions of people. Only Vietnam claims more speakers in Southeast Asia. Khmer's closest language relatives are Thai and Lao, which developed from Khmer and share a few common words. The language can be difficult for Westerners to learn, with its distinctive alphabet and many vowels and consonants, including some combination consonant-vowel symbols. Also, Khmer uses special mannerisms and vocabulary, depending on who is having the conversation. Peasants speak to each other in entirely different ways, and even use different vocabulary, than when they speak to their social superiors like their elders, monks or, rarely, royalty.

Khmer literature ranges from folklore carved in ancient stone to modern stories told by survivors of the Khmer Rouge genocide. *The Reamker*, a famous Cambodian epic poem, is often told in rhyming verses and accompanied by special dances that help bring the story to life. Reamker stories are carved on the walls of Angkor Wat, and acted out in nang sbek, shadow plays using black leather puppets. Religious stories like jakatas—stories of Buddha's other lives, in which he performed selfless acts while he lived a former, lower life as an animal—are popular. Cambodia's king Ang Duong, who ruled from 1841 to 1860, wrote elegant versions of jakata tales that remain favorites.

Hun Sen dedicates many new schools in rural areas each year, and reports that 90% of eligible Cambodian children complete elementary school. But most Cambodian families struggle to achieve even that modest level of education. Cambodia only spends 2.6% of its national profits on education for its children—one of the 20 lowest expenditures in the world. Elementary schools can only afford one teacher per 47 students on average. Tired of waiting for the government to pay their already low salaries, many teachers charge students a fee for coming to class. Add that to the cost of buying proper books and supplies, and the cost of getting to school, especially in rural areas, quickly moves beyond the means of the average Cambodian family of poor farmers. It's no wonder that most families pull their kids out of school after 5th grade to help on the family farm. Only 47% of eligible children enroll in middle and high school, and less than 15% go on to attend

**FYI FACT:**

**A quick lesson in Khmer**

**Hello** — suosdey

**How are you?** — Sok sebai

**Goodbye** — chumree-uhp lee-uh

**Thank you** — awkun

**What is that?** — nuh keu uhvuh-ee

**Where is the hotel?** — Oata-el nuh-oo a-e na

**Where is the restaurant?** — Hang baee nuh-oo a-e na

**I want to learn to dance the Ramvong.** — kh'nyom chawng ree-uhn ro-am ro-am vu-uhng

**I'm off to Phnom Penh on my bike!** — Me chi kong Phnom Penh

**Sources:** Omniglot, "Useful Phrases in Khmer"
http://www.omniglot.com/language/phrases/khmer.php

Daniel White, *Frommer's Cambodia and Laos* (Hoboken: New Jersey: Wiley Publishing, 2010), pp. 325-327.

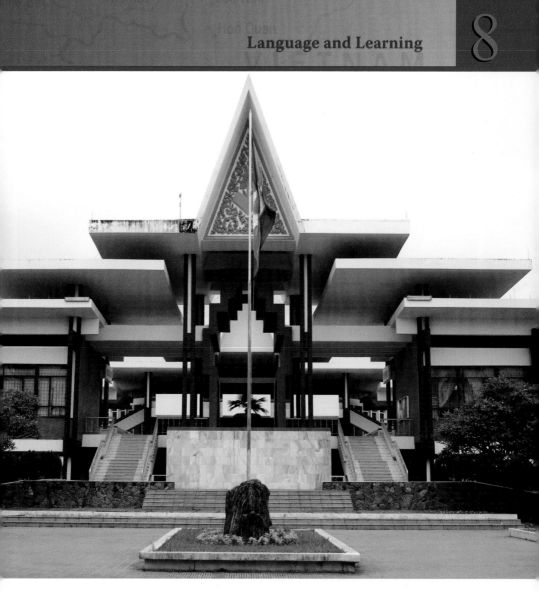

**Founded in 1960, the Royal University of Phnom Penh is Cambodia's oldest and largest university. The Khmer Rouge shut it down for several years during the 1970s, and it reopened in 1980.**

a university.[1] Only three out of every four of Cambodia's adults could read and write in 2009, and most experts suspect that that literacy rate is much lower in rural areas.[2] Wealthy parents usually pay big money to send their children to boarding schools abroad, especially when it comes to a university education. The Royal University of Phnom Penh is Cambodia's largest and has the best reputation, but it can only offer a basic education to its 15,000 students when so few Cambodians are qualified to teach.[3]

King Norodom Sihamoni led all Cambodians in celebration of the nation's 60th Independence Day on November 9, 2013, with fireworks, parties, and a grand parade through Phnom Penh.

# Famous Cambodians

**Norodom Sihanouk** (1922–2012) was crowned king by the German-controlled French government when he was only 18 years old. The self-described "naughty boy" enjoyed French wines, wrote music, and studied movies. He also married six times and had at least 14 children. After being named prime minister and king several different times, Sihanouk appears in the *Guinness Book of World Records* for having held the most political offices of anyone in the world.

Like many children of Cambodia's elite, King Sihanouk's son, **Norodom Sihamoni** (1953– ), spent his childhood away from Cambodia, studying at prestigious boarding schools in Czechoslovakia. He lived in France for almost 20 years, teaching ballet and classical Cambodian dance. Unlike his popular and outspoken father, who spent his life chasing either politics or pretty ladies, the quiet, unmarried, and childless Sihamoni mostly keeps to himself in the palace today.

**Hun Sen** (1952– ) was born to a peasant family in Kampong Cham. He began studying in a monastery when he was 13, but left to join the Khmer Rouge as a soldier in 1970, even lying about his age so that people would think that he was old enough to fight. He lost his left eye to the violence in 1975, and today has a glass one. Hun Sen's oldest son, Hun Manet, graduated from the U.S. Military Academy at West Point, New York in 1999.

**Actors Brad Pitt and Angelina Jolie attend the world premiere of the movie *World War Z* with their sons Maddox (left, 12 years old) and Pax (right, 10 years old). Cambodian native Maddox scored a small role in the movie—as a zombie!—alongside his dad.**

American actress **Angelina Jolie** first traveled to Cambodia to act in *Lara Croft: Tomb Raider*, a 2001 movie based on a popular video game. Shooting scenes around the Angkor Wat temple complex, Jolie was shocked to see the living conditions of the Cambodian poor. She adopted an infant Cambodian orphan in 2002, **Maddox Jolie-Pitt**, and built a traditional home—on stilts—in the Cambodian jungle. Today she is a dedicated mother and a respected spokeswoman for the United Nations on human rights issues, especially on behalf of developing countries like Cambodia. Through the Maddox Jolie-Pitt Foundation, she provides donations and manpower to support the Samlaut National Park in the Cardamom Mountains, the last remaining tropical rainforest in northwestern Cambodia. King Sihamoni awarded Jolie Cambodian citizenship in 2005.

Forced into the Khmer Rouge army as a child, **Aki Ra** (ca. 1970– ) used his small hands to craft and lay land mines throughout Cambodia. Today, he uses that same expertise to find and disarm the deadly devices he was once forced to lay. At first he just used a stick and his wits; now he has U.N. training and specialized hand tools. Thanks to the work of Aki Ra and other deminers, the number of red signs with skull-and-crossbones markings reminding villagers to beware of land mines drops each year. Injuries due to land mine explosions have also decreased, from over 800 every year, to around 400 in 2006. Aki Ra and his wife also run the Cambodian Land Mine Museum near Siem Reap, where entrance fees pay for an orphanage and school for Cambodian children affected by land mines.

**Aki Ra formed the Self Help Cambodian Demining Group. To date, the organization has disabled about 50,000 mines and other land-based weapons. Ra's life story is featured in the 2011 movie *A Perfect Soldier*.**

Towering over the heart of Phnom Penh, the temple of Wat Phnom is a favorite of Cambodians on Buddhist holy days. The large garden clock below the temple is a gift of friendship from the countries of France and China.

Chapter

# 10

# We Visit
# Cambodia

Exotic, historic, mysterious, lush. If you are ready for adventure, Cambodia is ready to take your breath away. Most tourists experience a whole world of sights, sounds, and smells in Cambodia's top three destinations: Phnom Penh, Siem Reap, and Sihanoukville.

Phnom Penh, the capital and largest city, teems with 2.2 million people. Legend has it that Phnom Penh got its modern name from Old Lady Penh, who found sacred statues inside a floating log in 1434. Wat Penh stands in honor of the shrine she created to the statues. Before you go into this sacred house, show respect for Cambodia's spiritual heritage by taking off your shoes, and making sure you are dressed modestly, hot weather or not. Enjoy more of Cambodia's history at the National Museum, a treasure house of ancient Khmer artifacts, wat statues, and cultural exhibits. Be sure to linger to take in a production of colorful traditional dances at the adjoining Plae Pakaa theater.

Phnom Penh did not become the permanent capital of Cambodia until 1866, when King Norodom I built his home there. The French occupation built Phnom Penh into the glorious city it is today. The French constructed beautiful colonial-era buildings, including magnificent mansions that a few wealthy government ministers still call home. The Sisowath Quay riverfront still bustles with French culture. Grab a simple treat like coffee and a baguette, then take a river cruise to see the opulent, gilded Royal Palace, which you can also visit when back on land. Indulge in a snack from a cart, like a tokolok—an icy cold smoothie made from your choice of fruit blended with sweetened condensed milk—or haggle street vendors to buy a traditional karma. This is a large scarf that all Cambodians wear as a bandanna, skirt, or even use as a towel or hammock.

Phnom Penh seems like a tourist's paradise, a perfect blend of jungle heat and sunshine, history, beauty, and exotic fun. It's easy to forget that just outside the city, the Killing Fields (Choeung Ek) and the Tuol Sleng Genocide Museum serve as silent reminders of the city's brutal past at the hands of the Khmer Rouge. As many as 30,000 prisoners were led to Tuol Sleng, Pol Pot's secret prison. Only six are known to have survived. Throughout the country, Cambodians remind themselves of that dark time in quiet ways, like shrines built of skulls or bones left scattered on the ground.

Paved roads through the capital city lead to six national highways radiating out from Phnom Penh like spokes on a wheel. But Western-style transportation outside of the city, where few people can afford cars—or Phnom Penh's favorite, motorbikes—gets much trickier. Dirt roads dominate and potholed roads lie in disrepair from their damage after the war. Traveling can get very dusty during the dry season. During the monsoon season, roads become so muddy as to be almost impassable. Thanks to wealthy tourist traffic, two of these main roads stay in good shape year-round—national highway 6 to Siem Reap, and national highway 4 to Sihanoukville.

The town of Siem Reap in Cambodia's central-west, on the north shore of the Tonle Sap, serves as a base for tourists visiting one of the grandest and most mysterious temple sites in the world. For many people, Angkor Wat is the highlight of a trip to Cambodia or even Southeast Asia.[1] Where once a great city teemed with Buddhist monks and priests, and was devoted to fulfilling every wish of Jayavarman VII, today the temples bear the scars of time as they sit quietly in the jungle. The Bayon of Angkor Thom, built around 1190 CE, is a temple with enormous faces of the god-king Jayavaraman VII carved from rock. The Prohm temple remains as the French found it, with the roots of fig trees wrapped around pillars, strangling statues and obscuring carvings. The screech of wild monkeys makes this interaction of man and nature timeless and exotic, especially if you bring enough money to see it from the back of an elephant.

Sihanoukville is a young city, founded by King Norodom Sihanouk after Cambodia's independence from the French as a port for deep-water trading ships on the Gulf of Thailand. It is perched on a peninsula on Kampong Saom Bay, with pristine islands a quick boat ride away. Mellow locals dish out delicious seafood, especially crab, seasoned to perfection with spices grown in nearby Kampot, a town world-famous for its pepper.[2] With the coast's postcard-perfect sandy beaches, it is no surprise that the nearby town of Kep was once a royal seaside resort. Today anyone can stay at modern hotels to enjoy the relaxed seaside vibe framed by palm trees and blue skies. The Koh Kong Conservation Corridor, just to the north in the Cardamom Range, makes a great side trip from the beach for ecotourists who want to experience a rainforest whose secrets are just now being discovered.

Most of Cambodia's visitors zip among these "big three" sites, then hop back on a plane for home, their senses filled with the sweet warm tropics, their eyes opened to a new land of history and wonder. But step off the beaten path if you really want to see Cambodia. Do as the locals do and rent your own motorbike, or even bring along your bike and pedal the dirt highways for a trip you'll never forget.

Journey northwest and enjoy scenic mountain parks that protect sacred temples, with far fewer crowds than Angkor Wat. In the Dangrek

**Resorts along Sihanoukville's white-sand beaches offer views of the Gulf of Thailand's turquoise waters.**

**A waterfall in Phnom Kulen National Park, located in the northwest part of Cambodia**

Mountains in northwestern Cambodia, visit the cascading waterfalls of Phnom Kulen to see the shrine where Jayavarman II declared himself a god-king in 802 CE. Another treasure on the Thai border is Preah Vihear, a lichen-covered stone temple perched atop a low mountain. The temple's proximity to the Thai border led to an ugly border dispute, with both sides claiming the site as their own to cash in on tourism dollars when the U.N. protected it as a World Heritage Site.

Next, head to the western farming center of Battambang. Seeing its sprawling rice paddies, you would never know it is Cambodia's second-largest city, with 250,000 people. The slower pace of life here is echoed throughout the ringed lowland of Cambodia. Like a trip through a time machine, Cambodia's villages have looked the same for a thousand years, built by hand from natural materials like wood, woven leaves, and handmade clay-tile roofs. Stilts prop up the houses, a protection from flooding during the rainy season, and a natural cooling technique during the hot, dry season. Without electricity, villagers have no refrigerators, no telephones, no air conditioning. Families sleep together on the floor at night on woven mat beds, which are rolled up in the morning and put away so the floor can be used for meals. These are prepared in handmade clay pots over hot coals. Livestock like water buffalo and oxen graze below the house. In the dry season, the family might sleep next to them in hammocks in a special hut away from the house to prevent fires.[3]

Make a little eye contact, smile, and wave, and you will discover Cambodia's real treasure—its people. Despite their repeated hardships, Cambodians remain friendly, upbeat, warm, and welcoming. Should you be lucky enough to be invited into a Cambodian home for dinner, your host will greet you with a grin and a bow, his hands held together in a prayer position over his heart. Mirror his gesture and take off your shoes. The lovely smell that greets you may be freshly cut jasmine

**FYI FACT:**

Fried spider is a special delicacy you can buy from snack carts in Phnom Penh. Vendors catch Thai zebra tarantulas, toss them with spices, garlic, and oil, then fry them.

flowers, or a simmering pot of fish stew. Elderly members of the family live next door or in the same house, so they are always available to share a joke or a conversation. Don't be surprised if friends and neighbors drop in for a visit and stay for dinner.

Come and sit at a table with plates and chopsticks or spoons in the city, or join your hosts on the floor along the edge of a mat for a traditional Cambodian village meal. As the guest, you are served the best food the family has. Cambodian food shows a deliciously complicated history of Indian, Chinese, and French influences, prepared simply and with fewer spices than in neighboring countries. Naturally, there will be rice. Cambodians prepare many varieties of rice, and in many ways. A favorite way is rolling the rice into balls so it can be eaten with your fingers. In fact, everything at the table—fish, meat, eggs, vegetables—might be cut into bite-sized pieces to make it easier to scoop up with your right hand. If soup is served, you can use a spoon, or just slurp up the broth from the bowl. Delicious desserts couldn't be simpler—sweet, fresh bananas, mangos, jackfruit, or durian can be picked from trees right outside the door.

After dinner in the city, you might go roller skating or bowling. Karaoke is becoming very popular, even in smaller towns. Costly movie theaters have largely fallen into disrepair over the years, but even villagers enjoy TV from time to time. The few who own TV sets power them with a car battery, and gather all their neighbors together to watch a show on one of Cambodia's nine channels. In the country, join a Cambodian family for a bike ride, a card game, or a sport like volleyball, badminton, or soccer. As night falls, try your hand at learning the magic and fun of the Ramvong dance by lantern light. What a perfect way to remember that, despite their years of violence, war, and unrest, the Khmers will continue to live on for another thousand years, laughing and celebrating their rich past together.

# Amok

## (Khmer Fish Stew)

This creamy, slightly sweet fish stew is sometimes considered the national dish of Cambodia. Khmer cooks use kroeung, a mixture of natural spices ground into a paste, to flavor almost everything. Kroeung can be as individual as the person making it, but always includes ingredients naturally found in Cambodia, like lemongrass, turmeric, kaffir lime leaves, garlic, and exotic roots like galangal and krachai. Trek to your nearest Asian grocery store for authentic ingredients. If you can't find pre-made kroeung, look for another jar of curry paste (as well as fish sauce) in the international section of most supermarkets.

**Ingredients:**
2 tablespoons canola oil
2 tablespoons kroeung (Khmer curry paste), or another curry paste
1 pound tilapia fillet, sliced thinly
3 cups bok choy, sliced thinly
1 can (15 ounces) coconut milk
1 teaspoon brown sugar
4 tablespoons fish sauce
Hot cooked rice (four servings)
Banana leaves (optional)

**Instructions:**
Prepare the following recipe with adult supervision:
1. Heat the oil in a skillet on medium heat. Add the curry paste and cook, stirring frequently, until browned (about five minutes).
2. Add the sliced fish and bok choy to the skillet. Cook, stirring frequently, until the leaves begin to wilt.
3. Add the coconut milk, sugar, and fish sauce and stir to combine.
4. Bring mixture just to a boil, then remove from heat. Divide rice into four bowls. Ladle the stew over the rice. If desired, garnish with banana leaves. Serve immediately.

Adapted from Joannès Rivère, *Cambodian Cooking* (Singapore: Periplus, 2008), p. 55.

Cambodians appreciate the simple, resourceful, and useful. They craft mats from reeds, grasses, or even scraps of old clothes to use as placemats, rugs, or beds and tables. Make your own placemat-sized mat, just like a Cambodian would, by using this simple weaving technique.

# Hand-Woven Mat

## Materials
- Placemat-sized piece of sturdy cardboard
- Ruler
- Pencil
- Scissors
- Tape
- String or weaving material (twine, yarn, plastic string, or even old t-shirts cut into long, even strips)

## Instructions

1. Using the pencil and ruler, make a mark every ½ inch across one long edge of the cardboard. Repeat on the other long edge. Cut ~½-inch slits down from the edge at each mark.
2. Hold your cardboard in a placemat orientation. Thread a single string through the top left slit, leaving a bit of loose end dangling. Tape the loose end to one face of the cardboard. This will be the "back" of the mat.
3. From your starting point in step 2, wind the string straight down the placemat and thread it through the leftmost bottom slit and to the back. Bring the string to the front through the slit immediately to the right, then straight up across the placemat, threading it to the back of the mat through the slit next to where you started. Note: You will make a pattern, creating long vertical bars on the "front" of your mat, and short horizontal lines that connect the slits on the "back."
4. Repeat step 3 until all the slits have been used. Trim and tape the extra string to the back of the cardboard (as in step 2).
5. Tape a new string to the back of the bottom left side of the cardboard. On the free end of the string, make a shoelace-style cap around the end with a piece of tape.
6. Starting at the bottom of the placemat, weave the string from step 5 over and under the bars you have made, going from the left side to the right. After you pass the last bar, start a new row on top of the one you just made by weaving back the opposite way.
7. If you begin to run out of string, tie on a new length of string to the free end of your weaving string. Make a new tape-covered end.
8. Continue until your placemat is filled with rows of woven string.
9. Gently remove the tape from the back of the placemat. Gently remove the loops from the slits. Working from one end to the other, pull the loops gently to tighten your weaving. Tie a knot in each of the four loose ends and trim them. Enjoy your new mat!

57

# TIMELINE

**Dates BCE**

| | |
|---|---|
| **5200** | Earliest evidence of people in Cambodia. |
| **2500** | Rice cultivation in Cambodia begins. |

**Dates CE**

| | |
|---|---|
| **180** | The Empire of Funan arises and lasts until the 6th century. |
| **500s–802** | The Kingdom of Chenla begins and lasts until 802. |
| **611** | The first known use of the Khmer language. |
| **802** | Jayavarman II establishes the Khmer Empire. |
| **12th century** | The Angkor temple complex, including Angkor Wat, is built. |
| **1434** | Phnom Penh is founded. |
| **1772** | Siamese warriors invade Cambodia. |
| **1835–1840** | Vietnam defeats Siam and occupies Cambodia. |
| **1863** | The French take over Cambodia and rule it as a colony for the next 90 years. |
| **1927** | Sisowath Monivong ascends the throne after his father, King Sisowath, dies. |
| **1941** | King Sisowath Monivong dies and his grandson Norodom Sihanouk is crowned king; Japanese occupy Cambodia until their defeat at the end of World War II in 1945. |
| **1946** | France re-establishes control, but also helps Cambodia towards independence. |
| **1947** | Cambodia holds elections for the first National Assembly. |
| **1953** | The Kingdom of Cambodia declares its independence from France. |
| **1965** | Sihanouk allows the Communist North Vietnamese to use Cambodian military bases in their fight against South Vietnam. |
| **1970** | Lon Nol overthrows Sihanouk in a military coup and creates the Khmer Republic; he allows U.S. troops to occupy eastern Cambodia during the Vietnam War. |
| **1975** | The Khmer Rouge overthrow Lon Nol and Pol Pot becomes prime minister of the country, which he names Democratic Kampuchea. |
| **1978** | Vietnam invades Cambodia and defeats the Khmer Rouge, creating the People's Republic of Kampuchea. Hundreds of thousands of Cambodians live in refugee camps, near death from starvation and abuse. |
| **1985** | Hun Sen is named prime minister of Cambodia. |
| **1989** | Vietnamese troops leave Cambodia. Hun Sen renames the country the State of Cambodia. |
| **1991** | Cambodia's warring political groups sign the Paris Peace Accords. |
| **1992** | United Nations Transitional Authority takes control of Cambodia to pave the way for free elections and a new constitution. |
| **1993** | Prince Ranariddh, son of King Sihanouk, wins the U.N.-sponsored election and becomes "first" prime minister; Hun Sen is named "second" prime minister. |
| **1995** | Sam Rainsy, a former finance minister, forms the Khmer Nation political party to call attention to corruption throughout the government. |
| **1998** | Pol Pot dies in hiding. The last remaining Khmer Rouge troops surrender. |
| **2004** | King Sihanouk abdicates the throne. His son, Sihamoni, is named king. |

| 2008 | Hun Sen's Communist People's Party again wins National Assembly elections despite claims of voter fraud. |
| 2010 | Former Khmer Rouge leader Kaing Guek Eav is found guilty of crimes against humanity and sentenced to life in prison. |
| 2012 | Former king Norodom Sihanouk dies of a heart attack at age 89. |
| 2014 | The United States agrees to provide $27.4 million to Cambodia in aid of improving health services. |

# CHAPTER NOTES

**Introduction**
1. United Nations Development Policy and Analysis Division, "Least Developed Countries," http://www.unohrlls.org/en/ldc/25/

**Chapter 1. The People of the Naga**
1. I. G. Edmonds, *The Khmers of Cambodia: The Story of a Mysterious People* (Indianapolis: Bobbs-Merrill, 1970), p. 14.
2. David Chandler, A History of Cambodia. 3rd Edition (Boulder, Colorado: Westview Press, 2000), p. 9.
3. World Bank, "Cambodia," http://www.worldbank.org/en/country/cambodia
4. Ibid.
5. United Nations World Food Programme, http://www.wfp.org/countries/cambodia/overview

**Chapter 2. Geography**
1. Cambodia, Weatherbase.com http://www.weatherbase.com/weather/city.php3?c=KH

**Chapter 3. Ancient History to Cambodian Independence**
1. David Chandler, *A History of Cambodia*, 3rd Edition (Boulder, CO: Westview Press, 2000), p. 9.
2. Daniel White, *Frommer's Cambodia & Laos* (Hoboken, NJ: Wiley Publishing, Inc., 2010), p. 12.
3. Damian Evans, et al, "A Comprehensive Archaeological Map of the World's Largest Preindustrial Settlement Complex at Angkor, Cambodia," Proceedings of the National Academy of the Sciences of the United States of America, September 4, 2007, vol. 104, no. 36, pp. 14277–14282.

**Chapter 4. Modern History**
1. Daniel White, *Frommer's Cambodia & Laos* (Hoboken, NJ: Wiley Publishing, 2010), p. 10.

**Chapter 5. Government and Politics**
1. Joel Brinkley, *Cambodia's Curse: The Modern History of a Troubled Land* (New York: Public Affairs, 2001), p. xiv.
2. Transparency International, "Cambodia – Country Profile," http://www.transparency.org/country#KHM
3. Samean Yun, "Hun Sen Defends Son's Nomination," translated by Rachel Vandenbrink. Radio Free Asia, March 7, 2013.

**Chapter 6. Resources and Jobs**
1. Asian Development Bank, "Cambodia and ADB," http://www.adb.org/countries/cambodia
2. Ministry of Tourism, "Tourism Statistics Report," Statistics and Information Department, Kingdom of Cambodia, February 2013. http://www.tourismcambodia.org/mot/index.php?view=statistic_report
3. Public Broadcasting Service, "Cambodia Garment Worker Justice," Religion and Ethics Weekly, May 18, 2012, http://www.pbs.org/wnet/religionandethics/2012/05/18/may-18-2012-cambodia-garment-worker-justice/11033/

4. Ibid.
5. United States Central Intelligence Agency, "Cambodia," The World Factbook. October 25, 2013. https://www.cia.gov/library/publications/the-world-factbook/geos/cb.html
6. "Cambodia's Oil Resources: Blessing or Curse?" The Economist, February 26, 2009, http://www.economist.com/node/13184945
7. "Cambodia," The World Factbook.
8. World Bank, "Cambodia," http://www.worldbank.org/en/country/cambodia
9. Ek Chanboreth, "Aid Effectiveness in Cambodia," Wolfensohn Center for Development at the Brookings Institute, December 2008, p. 4.
10. Guy De Launey, "Cambodia's Riel Survives Alongside the Dollar," BBC News, March 30, 2011.

**Chapter 7. Religion and Holidays**
1. CultureGrams, *Asia and Oceania* (Provo, Utah: Axiom Press, 2010), p. 38.
2. Ibid., p. 40.

**Chapter 8. Language and Learning**
1. World Bank, "Cambodia." http://www.worldbank.org/en/country/cambodia
2. Ibid.
3. Royal University of Phnom Penh, http://www.rupp.edu.kh

**Chapter 10. We Visit Cambodia**
1. Daniel White, *Frommer's Cambodia & Laos* (Hoboken, NJ: Wiley Publishing, Inc., 2010), p. 7.
2. Ibid., p. 2.
3. Lim Hak Kheang, Madeline Elizabeth Ehrman, and Kem Sos, *Contemporary Cambodia: The Social Institutions* (Washington, DC: Foreign Service Institute, 1974), p. 87.

# FURTHER READING

**Books**

Carrison, Muriel Paskin. *Cambodian Folk Stories from the Gatiloke*. Boston: Tuttle Publishing, 2011.
Linda Crew. *Children of the River*. New York: Laurel-Leaf, 1989.
Goldstein, Margaret J. *Cambodia in Pictures: Visual Geography*. Minneapolis: Lerner Publications, 2004.
Ho, Mingfong. *The Clay Marble*. New York: Farrar, Straus, and Giroux, 1993.
Kras, Sarah Louise. *Cambodia: Enchantment of the World*. Danbury, Conn.: Children's Press, 2005.
Pastore, Clare. *A Voyage from Cambodia from 1975*. New York: Berkeley Jam Books, 2001.
Sheehan, Sean and Barbara Cooke. *Cambodia*. Tarrytown, New York: Marshall Cavendish Benchmark, 2007.
Weltig, Matthew Scott. *Pol Pot's Cambodia*. Minneapolis: Twenty-First Century Books, 2009.


**On the Internet**

Buddhist Library and Meditation Centre: Project Cambodia
    http://www.buddhistlibrary.org.au/project-cambodia/information
Cambodia Travel Guides
    http://www.canbypublications.com/
King Norodom Sihamoni Official Website
    http://www.norodomsihamoni.org/front_e.htm
Tourism Cambodia, official website of the Ministry of Tourism
    http://www.tourismcambodia.com
World Wildlife Foundation: Cambodia
    http://cambodia.panda.org/

# WORKS CONSULTED

Asian Development Bank. "Cambodia and ADB." http://www.adb.org/countries/cambodia

Brinkley, Joel. *Cambodia's Curse: The Modern History of a Troubled Land*. New York: Public Affairs, 2001.

British Broadcasting Company News. "Cambodia Profile – Timeline." March 17, 2013. http://www.bbc.co.uk/news/world-asia-pacific-13006828

"Cambodia's Oil Resources: Blessing or Curse?" *The Economist*, February 26, 2009. http://www.economist.com/node/13184945

Chanboreth, Ek. "Aid Effectiveness in Cambodia." Wolfensohn Center for Development at the Brookings Institute, December 2008.

Chandler, David. *A History of Cambodia*. 3rd Edition. Boulder, CO: Westview Press, 2000.

Cornfield, Justin. *The History of Cambodia*. Santa Barbara, CA: Greenwood Press, 2009.

De Launey, Guy. "Cambodia's Riel Survives Alongside the Dollar." BBC News, March 30, 2011.

Edmonds, I. G. *The Khmers of Cambodia: The Story of a Mysterious People*. Indianapolis: The Bobbs-Merrill Company, Inc., 1970.

Evans, Damian, Christophe Pottier, Roland Fletcher, Scott Hensley, Ian Tapley, Anthony Milne, and Michael Barbetti. "A Comprehensive Archaeological Map of the World's Largest Preindustrial Settlement Complex at Angkor, Cambodia." *Proceedings of the National Academy of the Sciences of the United States of America*, September 4, 2007, vol. 104, no. 36, pp. 14277–14282.

Fuller, Thomas. "A Spectacle of Mourning for a King in Cambodia." *New York Times*, February 1, 2013.

Gray, Dennis. "Cambodia's king seen as a 'prisoner' in his palace." NBCNews.com, May 29, 2011. http://www.nbcnews.com/id/43209362/ns/world_news-asia_pacific/t/cambodias-king-prisoner-his-palace/#.UYt1Ko4aDN4

Hude, Felix. "Biking Southeast Asia with Mr. Pumpy!" http://www.mrpumpy.net/index.html

Jenkins, Mark. "The Healing Fields." *National Geographic*, January 2012. http://ngm.nationalgeographic.com/ 2012/01/landmines/jenkins-text

Ministry of Tourism. "Tourism Statistics Report." Statistics and Information Department, Kingdom of Cambodia, February 2013. http://www.tourismcambodia.org/mot/index.php?view=statistic_report.

Public Broadcasting Service. "Cambodia Garment Worker Justice." *Religion and Ethics Weekly*. May 18, 2012. http://www.pbs.org/wnet/religionandethics/episodes/may-18-2012/cambodia-garment-worker-justice/11033/

Rivère, Joannès. *Cambodian Cooking*. Singapore: Periplus, 2008.

Royal University of Phnom Penh. http://www.rupp.edu.kh

Sihamoni, Norodom. "Royal Decree on Designation of Animals and Plants as National Symbols of the Kingdom of Cambodia." March 21, 2005. http://www.forestry.gov.kh/Documents/ROYAL-DECREE-ENG.pdf

Transparency International. "Cambodia – Country Profile." http://www.transparency.org/country#KHM

United States Central Intelligence Agency. "Cambodia." *The World Factbook*. https://www.cia.gov/library/publications/the-world-factbook/geos/cb.html

Weatherbase. Cambodia. http://www.weatherbase.com/weather/city.php3?c=KH

White, Daniel. *Frommer's Cambodia & Laos*. Hoboken, New Jersey: Wiley Publishing, 2010.

World Bank. "Cambodia Home." http://www.worldbank.org/en/country/cambodia

Yun, Samean. "Hun Sen Defends Son's Nomination," Radio Free Asia. March 7, 2013, translated by Rachel Vandenbrink. http://www.rfa.org/english/news/cambodia/election-03072013191801.html

PHOTO CREDITS: Cover, pp. 1, 2 (bottom), 6–7, 8, 11, 13, 14, 18, 20, 38, 53, 57–Photos.com; pp. 2–3, 3, 7 (map), 10, 13 (flag), 16, 37, 45, 50, 54, 56–cc-by-sa; pp. 2 (top), 30–Mak Remissa/EPA/Newscom; p. 12–Central Intelligence Agency; p. 17–Philippe Lissac/Godong/picture-alliance/Newscom; pp. 22, 29–Tang Chhin Sothy/AFP/Getty Images; p. 24–Philippe Lopez/AFP/Newscom; p. 26–Kyodo News/AP Images; p. 27–AFP/Newscom; p. 28–National Museum of the U.S. Air Force; p. 33–William Ng/U.S. Department of State; p. 34–Florian Kopp/Westend61 GmbH/Newscom; p. 41–Heng Sinith/EPA/Newscom; p. 42–Natasha Graham/Global Partnership of Education; p. 46–Sovannara/Xinhua/Photoshot/Newscom; p. 48–Dave M. Benett/WireImage for Paramount/Getty Images; p. 49–DVS iPhoto Inc./Newscom. Every effort has been made to locate all copyright holders of material used in this book. If any errors or omissions have occurred, corrections will be made in future editions of the book.

**abdicate** (AB-dih-kayt)—To give up the rights and responsibilities of being a king or queen.

**animism** (AN-uh-miz-uhm)—Belief that objects in nature, like plants or animals, have souls.

**biodiversity** (bi-oh-dih-VUHR-sih-tee)—An environment with many different species of organisms.

**corruption** (kor-RUP-shun)—Dishonesty in the government.

**coup d'etat** (koo-day-TAH)—The sudden revolution, often by military force, that changes the leadership of a government.

**deminers** (dee-MY-nehrs)—People who remove land mines from a particular area.

**genocide** (JEN-oh-side)—The planned killing of a race or class of people.

**guerrilla** (goo-RILL-uh)—A soldier who fights a larger, more organized force with unconventional ways, like sneak attacks or homemade weapons.

**land mines** (LAND MINEZ)—Small explosive devices buried in the ground that detonate from the pressure of footsteps.

**malnourished** (mal-NOO-risht)—Underfed to the point of sickness.

**monsoon** (mon-SOON)—Heavy seasonal rain.

**non-governmental organizations** (NGOs)—Groups that work to help a country's people without using government money or resources.

**pristine** (priss-TEEN)—Unspoiled; in its original condition.

**proximity** (prawk-SIH-muh-tee)—Closeness in space or time.

# INDEX

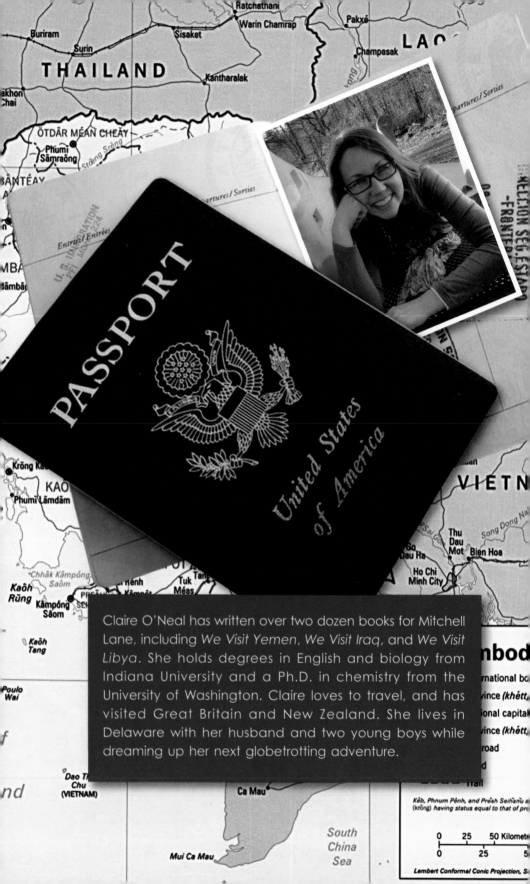

Claire O'Neal has written over two dozen books for Mitchell Lane, including *We Visit Yemen*, *We Visit Iraq*, and *We Visit Libya*. She holds degrees in English and biology from Indiana University and a Ph.D. in chemistry from the University of Washington. Claire loves to travel, and has visited Great Britain and New Zealand. She lives in Delaware with her husband and two young boys while dreaming up her next globetrotting adventure.